IN TRANSIT

by Roy Kimmel

illustrations by Nancy Haver
cartoon by Ian Kimmel

IN TRANSIT

ISBN: 978-0-9819820-5-2

Printed by Collective Copies
Amherst & Florence, Massachusetts

available from
Roy Kimmel
PO Box 159
Leverett, MA 01054
rik@crocker.com

For my grandmother who took me on my first bus trip

CONTENTS

BUS TRIPS AND BUS DRIVING

BUS DYNAMICS

EN ROUTE

INTRODUCTION

In the summer of 1987, my wife and I moved to Leverett, Massachusetts, a small hill town on the eastern edge of the Pioneer Valley. We were the third owners of a 200-year-old house, which had been the parsonage for the nearby Congregational Church since the 1820s. My wife had her own business, and I continued with my occasional freelance architectural model work but needed to supplement my income. I had retired from a good job in Passaic, New Jersey, where I ran a division for a company manufacturing bus stop shelters for transit authorities throughout the country. That's how I learned about buses and the day to day workings of public transportation.

A year after the move, a neighbor mentioned that a bus company in nearby Northampton needed part-time drivers, so, out of curiosity, I called and was asked to come in the next day. Thus began my bus driving career, lasting 23 years until mid 2011 when I decided to retire for the second time at the age of 75.

The first part of this book, **Bus Trips and Bus Driving**, is about bus trips I have taken since childhood and, for the past two dozen years, about my bus driving. This section of the book concludes with one of many bus trips my grandmother used to take, as described in her travel notes. In the second part, **Bus Dynamics**, I describe mechanical characteristics and idiosyncrasies of transit buses and coaches I have driven or ridden in and provide illustrations of the striking style of American buses built more than half a century ago. (A transit bus serves passengers at specific multiple stops along an urban or suburban route. A coach is a long distance or tour bus.) The third part, **En Route**, concludes with an idea of what public transportation and the urban environment might be like at the beginning of the next century.

I have been asked why I drive a bus. I enjoyed the tactility of driving anything since I was thirteen. The job of controlling a 40-foot bus might not be for everyone, but I discovered I had the disposition for it. The work keeps me alert and, at times, bus driving even seems therapeutic. The experience has made me a more patient person. It has been a good ride.

BUS TRIPS AND BUS DRIVING

1988

On a sunny October afternoon, I head for the bus company, Western Mass Bus Lines, across the Connecticut River in Northampton. I introduce myself to the dispatcher (herein referred to as "dispatch") who's sitting behind the counter. She asks for my driver's license and hands me an application. I fill it out in the ready room where several drivers – "operators" in transit speak – are chatting, waiting for their next shifts. Another is fast asleep on an old couch. I learn the company has a contract with the Pioneer Valley Transit Authority (PVTA), a regional transit authority based in Springfield. The company also has a school bus contract with the City of Northampton and owns eight coaches for charter work. I hand in the completed application, and dispatch asks me to stick around while she checks my driving and police records. All clean. A few minutes later, she tells me to climb into a transit bus parked out back and wait. I find the bus and help myself to the driver's seat. The engine is nearly 40 feet behind me. Driving this thing must be like driving a house. Soon a no-nonsense type of guy boards the bus and announces that he will be my trainer.

I was fortunate because at the time the company provided the training. The "circle check" is the first lesson – checking the bus to make sure everything is functioning properly before starting a route. For details about the circle check, see **Bus Dynamics**. After the circle-check session, the trainer tells me to pick up a stack of reading material for homework. The material includes the employee customer service guide for dealing professionally with the general public, information about safety issues, and mechanical details about the air-operated braking system. Passing a written test and demonstrating that I can drive a bus safely and confidently occur before the day I pick up my first passenger. The trainer's parting words are that every new bus driver will be "tested" by certain passengers. Most new bus drivers learn how to handle that after a little experience.

But first, a bus-trip memory, one of several to follow.

1944 BUS TRIP

I'm eight years old, and my father is overseas during the war. In late spring, my mother accepts a shipyard construction job in California. With her mother, my two younger brothers, and me, we head west from Virginia in her '41 Ford convertible to Birney, Montana, where a family friend owns a small cattle ranch. We're dropped off, and my mother continues on to Richmond, California, to learn welding for work in a shipyard turning out warships. She will be one of hundreds of thousands of women defense workers immortalized as Rosie the Riveter.

Near the end of the summer, my grandmother, brothers, and I board a bus in Sheridan, Wyoming, bound for Cheyenne, an all-night-and-day trip. The bus is a brawny front-engine rig built in the early 1930s. The wooden floorboard above the noisy transmission is missing, the drive shaft has a worn bearing, and the differential sounds as if it could use some fresh grease. During the war years, all public transport capable of running was pressed into service. Military personnel had priority, while civilians traveled on a space-available basis.

After some sleep, I awake at sunrise to see the light playing on the buttes as we rumble south along the dusty dirt road. Ten years later, I remembered that Wyoming coach while reading John Steinbeck's *The Wayward Bus*, in which he described an ancient bus with "The Power of Jesus" hand-painted atop its exposed front radiator.

Early afternoon we pull into the Cheyenne depot next to a bus that looks as if it was designed in the future. It has bright metal ribbing on the sides that wraps around the rear. The bus looks real keen. Waiting in the terminal for another bus to Salt Lake City, I stand around holding my kid's cowboy hat upside down. People start dropping nickels and dimes in the hat and when Grandmother comes out of the ladies' room, she scolds me for begging and confiscates the money. I whine I didn't know I was begging.

I'm disappointed the all-night bus to Salt Lake City is not the modernistic one I saw. I'm drifting in and out of sleep wondering how we are going to get over the distant mountains ahead. Later, as we climb, the driver is constantly changing gears. I dream I'm helping him.

Early next morning, the bus driver points out Devil's Slide, a huge trough sliced down a mountain with high jagged stones on both sides. My six-year-old brother explains to Grandmother, "Maybe God built the slide for the devil because the devil promised to be good." Some passengers and the driver overhear and laugh.

As we walk out of the terminal in Salt Lake City, the sky is bright, and I see the snow-capped mountains we came over during the night. Grandmother checks us into a downtown hotel, and we collapse on the beds because none of us slept on that noisy overnight bus. She wakes us at noon for an afternoon swim in Great Salt Lake. I remember how easy it was to float on the water because of all the salt.

Next morning we board a streamlined bus that looks like the one I saw in Cheyenne. I'm excited. A low step comes out when the door opens. I like the shape of the window on the door. The gear shift is on the steering column, like my mother's Ford. I settle into a seat near the front. A pretty woman steps on, offering pillows. A soldier across the aisle says, "Sure," with a wink. "How 'bout you, young fellow?" she asks me. I say in the deepest voice I can muster, "Sure", skipping the wink. The driver boards, looks around and says, "Morning, folks," and starts the bus. The engine is in the back and has a different kind of sound, smooth and fast-sounding, not the chugging noise of that old bus. The soldier sees I'm puzzled, and says, "That's a two-stroker, kid." I nod, pretending to understand. The soldier turns back to his *Li'l Abner* comic.

Our Silverside bus is bound for San Francisco. It's night coming into Nevada on US Route 50, but the bright moonlight makes the desert landscape between the mountain ranges appear white. In my half-sleep, I think I'm exploring a strange land as we growl westward.

After the Reno and Carson City stops early next morning, the bus slowly climbs from the hot plateau up to a mountain pass, then descends into the Lake Tahoe basin. We're dropped off at Zephyr Cove, about two miles from the California border, where we're going to be at a camp for the last two weeks of August. The place is rustic, the water is deep blue, and the mountains are high with snow on the ridges. I remember how the early morning sunrise reflected brilliant colors off the mountains. We fish, hike, ride horses, and sing-along by campfires at dusk. All seems right in the world, but I know this is not true: There's a war going on.

At the end of the month, we board an old bus like the one in Wyoming, bound for San Jose, California, an all-day trip down from the mountains on a winding road. From there we travel on a small more modern bus to nearby Los Gatos. I tell the woman driver I like her bus, and she tells me it's a Cruiserette. My brothers and I will be in a boarding school in Los Gatos until the end of the war.

Cruiserette

TRANSIT BUS AND SCHOOL BUS TRAINING

Transit bus A few days after I applied, the garage calls asking me to come in for bus-driving training. While a driver takes over dispatching, the dispatch woman and the regional head of a state agency that issues bus driver commercial licenses, are going to ride around in a 35-foot transit bus while I drive it. After adjusting the driver's seat and the outside mirrors, I start the bus, and while air pressure builds up, do the complete circle check. I forget to note that a little marker light at the top of the bus is out, and the agency man tells me to make a note of it on the defect card. This defect is not significant enough to keep the bus off the road. I stumble over my words doing the radio check. Dispatch tells me to think clearly about what I want to say before saying it, and also reminds me to fasten my seatbelt to avoid a $500 fine. I flip off the fast-idle switch and press the drive button, hearing a hiss of air as the transmission in back engages. Releasing the air-activated parking brake knob by pushing it down while my foot is on the brake pedal, I'm ready to roll. Dispatch and the agency man are seated several seats behind, pretending to ignore me unless I do something dumb.

As I release the brake, I immediately become aware of the bulk of the vehicle I'm steering. I put my faith in the outside mirrors as I guide the bus around the rotary just beyond the garage and out to a stop sign at the end of Industrial Drive. I have to turn left onto a busy city by-pass, with bumper-to-bumper traffic in both directions. Of course there is no traffic light, and it seems impossible to make the turn, but I don't want to spend 20 minutes trying to do it. Eventually, I ease out. This spot will be my least favorite part of the whole route, still two miles from the first passenger stop. After the turn, there is a railroad crossing. I turn on the four-way flashers, come to a full stop before the track, and open the front door so I can hear a train horn. No train. I shut the door, turn off the four-ways, and move across the rails making sure the rear of the bus is well clear before stopping again for traffic in front. After the next intersection, I accelerate up a hill, but the transmission doesn't shift. The engine seems to be revving at a feverish pitch. It's a two-cycle engine (same as "two-stroke", see page 54), so it just sounds fast. Eventually the transmission clunks into the next gear. As I enter a left-turn lane, I don't modulate the brake smoothly. Agency man looks up and reminds me I will be carrying people, not a load of lumber.

I'm reminded to glance constantly at both outside mirrors, like a bird glancing from side to side. In trusting those mirrors, I become less intimidated by the size of the bus. I get other reminders: observe what is near the bus; is a car crowding in or a pedestrian stepping off a curb?; keep well behind traffic because a 25-ton vehicle loaded with people needs plenty of distance to stop; look for brake lights coming on to anticipate slow-downs; be aware of a "stale" green traffic light, knowing it will change before the bus reaches the intersection. If you think you can beat the light before it changes, think again. The conscientious motorist in front will stop, and without a good following distance, the bus will not stop in time. If a car passes the bus only to brake as it tailgates the next car in front, back off. When waiting at a red light to cross or turn onto a busy highway, look both ways when the light changes before pulling out. Chances are a car will run a red light. Be aware of erratic motorists, and do not push the "right of way" issue. Dispatch and the agency man urge "go real slow" in tight situations like turns, approaching traffic, stop lights/signs, and bus stops.

We follow the regular route, with the destination sign set for "training." The stretch between Northampton and Amherst, home of the main campus of the University of Massachusetts (UMass), is a crowded, overbuilt highway. The bus stops are arbitrarily located, and I wonder how I will see them at night. At each bus stop, I pull over and open both front and rear doors. The right tires are about three inches from the curb. People attempt to board, but dispatch explains this bus is not in service. I'm reminded to check both doors to make sure no one is near before shutting them and pulling out. On the return trip, as we come down the slope of the Connecticut River bridge, heading back into Northampton, I modulate the brakes just right as we approach the changing traffic light. Dispatch exclaims, "Good stop!" I'm off to a good start. I'm beginning to feel confident, but cautioned not to feel over confident because any number of things can suddenly happen. Be relaxed, but be alert.

After we get back to the garage, I'm asked to watch training videos. Enacted scenes are of near-miss bus accidents and how to avoid them. One scene, viewed from the driver's seat, shows the driver signaling to pass a semi-truck on a multilane highway, making sure all is clear in the passing lane. After passing the truck, the bus pulls back into the right lane, not noticing a motorist merging into the same lane from an on-ramp hidden by the truck. An embarrassing swerve back into the passing lane avoids a sideswipe. Another scene shows a car passing a bus then suddenly jamming on its brakes to make a quick right turn, almost creating a rear-ender by the bus. Remembering the "plenty of following distance" rule, the driver slows down a little while the car is passing, in anticipation of this sort of thing. Yet another scene shows a transit bus signaling right to pull over at a bus stop. What the bus driver does not do is check the right mirror as a bicyclist is trying to pass the bus on the right. The cyclist stops and loudly curses. The least expected thing can happen, but we learn during training that near-misses and accidents are preventable. I'm asked if I would like to try driving a 40-foot transit bus. Sure, I say, what's an extra five feet? The trainer accompanies me for a short loop to nearby Easthampton. That extra five feet is a big difference, making the 35-footer seem darn right nimble. For more tips on bus driving, search Google for an audio of Bob Newhart's Bus Drivers School.

I'm asked to call the next day to set up some time for school bus training.

School bus A school bus is a truck with a yellow box on the frame. Driving a school bus differs from driving a transit bus. The front wheels are way out front. On a transit bus those wheels are behind the driver, so turning a corner in a school bus requires a different technique. If you steer a school bus into a side street as you would a transit bus, the front wheels will end up on the sidewalk of the street you are attempting to steer into. School buses have long rear overhangs which swing out away from the turning direction. Keeping an eye on the right outside mirror will minimize the chance that the rear right corner of the bus will smack into something like a utility pole when pulling out from a bus stop. I'm asked to drive a school bus over the next few days with a supervisor to cover the routes throughout the city and to learn where the school bus stops are. I get the hang of driving the bus, but I'm not sure I'll remember the stop locations in a city I don't know. I watch more videos at the garage about how to deal professionally with the kids, especially those junior high school ones. A typical scenario shows a group of seventh graders nagging the bus driver about something not allowed. The driver simply says it is not allowed, but the kids keep nagging. The driver again says it is not allowed. The kids stop nagging because the driver does not get drawn into any discussion. He simply repeats the same thing: it is not allowed. The kids give up and get on the bus.

SHIFTS

After a month of training several afternoons a week, I pass both the written and physical exams and am assigned badge number 7007. All the buses and employees at the Northampton garage are assigned 7000 series numbers, so I go by Double-0-Seven, a little perk. I'm issued a UFCW card: United Food and Commercial Workers Union local 1459. Bus drivers don't handle food for a living, but like a lot of organizations, unions diversify. The impetus for that union was the horrendous working conditions in the meat-packing slaughterhouses in the early days of the twentieth century. For more about that, read Upton Sinclair's *The Jungle* published in 1906.

Bus drivers, like all transportation workers, bid on the work shifts based on seniority, so the longer one is with the company, the better the chances of landing a desirable shift of one's choosing. The driver who has been with the company the longest bids first, then the next most senior person bids, and so on, down to the last person hired. The Northampton garage has a combination of full-time and part-time drivers, and all the full-timers bid before the part-timers. The most heavily travelled route is between Northampton and UMass/Amherst. During school semesters, there is a high frequency of service, but during the summer, Christmas, and various holidays, there is reduced service. A combination of full and part-time drivers work during the semesters, but mostly full-timers work during the reduced-service periods. Some part-timers also drive, filling in during vacation and sick days taken by the full-time people. Generally, the full-time drivers bid on routes that are close to a 40 hour week.

Bus driving is not a 9-to-5 job for all the drivers because it's not about a bunch of buses running together at the same time. Driving shifts are all over the dial. A typical full-time shift could go from 6 a.m. till 2 p.m. or from 1 p.m. till 9 p.m. A split-shift could go from 7 a.m. till 11 a.m. and from 2 p.m. till 6 p.m. Most full-time drivers don't like split-shifts, so those shifts usually go to the part-timers. Some part-timers, with enough seniority, choose a mid-day transit shift and drive a school bus before and after. The night owls take the late-night shifts, for example, from 7 p.m. till 3 a.m. As the newest part-time driver hired with the least seniority, I get the last shift available: two loops to Amherst/UMass in the late afternoon, two days a week (about eight hours), plus an afternoon school bus run those same days, just before the transit run.

1954 BUS TRIP

In the spring of 1954, my uncle in Lincoln, Nebraska, offers me a summer job for $23 a week, which I accept with glee. He owns a beer distribution business and a fleet of trucks to deliver the beer in the city and small towns up to 50 miles away. The name of the beer is Country Club, a name suggesting 1950's aspirations. I'm to be the truck driver's donkey, starting at 6:30 a.m., loading cases of beer into a truck, then off-loading them throughout 100-degree days into refrigerated tavern coolers. While I'm doing this, the driver buys rounds of Country Club for the tavern customers at the distributor's expense. Day customers are mostly retired farmers speaking Swedish or German. Deliveries are repeated every week to old, dark taverns in rural towns west of Lincoln. Many of those towns don't exist today because agribusiness has replaced many family farms, resulting in populations too sparse to support the towns. Heading east back to Lincoln on US Route 6 in the late afternoons, I could see the reflection of the sun off the copper dome of the 34-story state capitol 40 miles away.

At the beginning of the summer, I buy myself a $28.20 round-trip Greyhound ticket from Washington, DC, to Lincoln. We pull out late afternoon on a new bus with slanted side windows and air suspension. We pass through Frederick and Hagerstown, sleepy towns without the suburban sprawl that exists there today. Later, the driver works hard, shifting the gears as we climb into the Appalachians. We stop at a roadside greasy spoon called Eat At Joe's.

After a BLT sandwich, I board the bus along with the other passengers, and we pull back onto the mountain road. There's a man in the seat in front of me, his sleeveless undershirt arm draped over the top of his seat back. I get to see his arm pit. This, combined with a crying sick baby, makes for a sensory smorgasbord.

A man sitting next to me wearing a beat-up fedora hat kept telling me he was a federal man. Never explained why. I guessed maybe he was employed by the Civilian Conservation Corps twenty years before.

Late evening, we enter the Pennsylvania Turnpike. I overhear a man say that some day the whole country will be linked with these kinds of super highways. Before daylight next morning, I change buses in Pittsburgh, a Silverside coach bound for Cleveland. I grab a little sleep, waking up as we cruise north in the fog on a 1920s narrow concrete highway. I like the steady beat as we roll over the evenly spaced concrete expansion joints, a sound one rarely hears these days. We pass modest little houses almost touching the road, kitchen lights starting to come on. Traveling by Greyhound in those days brought one up close to America – families sitting on front porches at the end of a summer day, main intersections of small dusty towns, cornfields right up to the edge of the road.

We arrive in Cleveland with an hour to kill before the connection to Chicago. Time for fresh air, so I can enjoy a good breakfast for 89 cents in the terminal. In those days, city bus terminals were conveniently located downtown. Most were proudly built by Greyhound in the streamline modern architectural style prevalent from the early 1930s to the early '40s.

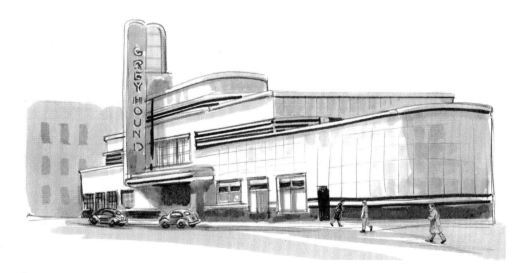

As we pull out of Cleveland in another Silverside, I see huge oscillating Hulett machines in the distance unloading ore boats. Soon we are traveling on Route 6 along the Lake Erie shore. Besides the usual flag stops where folks signal if they want to get on, the major stops are Sandusky and Toledo, in Ohio, and Gary, Indiana, where steel mills light up the overcast sky. In downtown Chicago, we pull into a new underground depot just in time to catch the overnighter to Omaha. Next morning, I change buses there and travel the final 60 miles to Lincoln in a late 1940s ACF–Brill coach.

Burma Shave advertising signs are placed sequentially in groups of six along the highway. Here are a few classics I jotted down during the trip.

> The midnight ride
> Of Paul
> For beer
> Led to a
> Warmer hemisphere
> *Burma Shave*
>
> Why is it
> When you
> Try to pass
> The guy in front
> Goes twice as fast
> *Burma Shave.*

When I arrive in Lincoln, my aunt meets me, saying I did well. She thinks most teenagers would not know how to make the trip arrangements. I didn't see why not.

ON THE JOB, THE FIRST DAY

I will not forget that first day, which came close to being my last day on the job. I do an afternoon school bus run from a vocational school, with a list of specific drop-off locations for the kids. Mind you, I don't know the Northampton streets yet. The kids board the bus, with vocal chords going full tilt. "Hey, new driver!" I think of the movie *Blackboard Jungle* where, at the beginning of school term, it's bedlam in the school auditorium until the hatchet-faced superintendent yells into the microphone, "SHADAP!" I'm tempted to yell the same thing but instead pick a volunteer who's not rowdy and ask him to give me directions. He says, "Oh absolutely, I like being helpful." Soon my volunteer kid says, "Turn right", "Go straight", "Turn left", "Stop here." One kid gets off. This scene is repeated enough times until I realize I'm dropping each kid off at his or her house instead of the designated drop-off locations. I swear I'll get a street map of the city and memorize the proper drop-off points. About a week before, I asked my teenage son what I should expect, driving a school bus. A few days later he produced this cartoon.

Because of the door-to-door delivery, I'm a little late getting back to the garage. I park the school bus, sweep it, and turn in the paper work. Dispatch says to get going because I'm late for my transit route. I fire up a 40-foot Grumman (see page 53), do the circle check, and drive the two miles to the beginning of the route at Smith College. For the first time in my life, I'm picking up passengers. The first two loops to UMass via Amherst go well.

Just because I talk about driving a bus right doesn't mean I'm not going to tell about my driving a bus wrong. Halfway through the third loop, it's pouring and dark outside, and condensation is building up on the right side of the front windshield. I turn right, heading for the main university bus stop, and hear "crunch". Somebody in the back of the bus yells, "Contact!" I stop, open the front door, and look back. I clipped a car that was illegally parked at the very corner of the narrow street I had turned into. Point of contact was just in front of the bus right rear wheel. I call dispatch on the radio and calmly state what happened, mentioning where the car was parked, continuing to say the bus pushed that car into another legally parked car. Dispatch is not happy, especially when she asks what I was doing out there in the first place. I was supposed to do two loops, not three. She calls the UMass police to investigate the accident. After the police complete their report, I change the destination sign to "out of service" and head straight back to the garage. After I fill out the accident report forms, dispatch says the manager would like to have a talk with me next morning, 7:00 sharp. Next morning, the manager asks if I had learned anything. I tell him the accident was probably preventable. He says, "Darn right, the accident was preventable! All accidents are preventable!"

It was not my last day on the job.

1955 BUS TRIP

While living with my parents in New Zealand, I, a State Department brat, am shipped off to a boarding school in Delaware. It was deemed that a prep school might straighten me out. This school owned a second-hand pre-war bus made by Flxible (no typo), painted cardinal red, the school color. It was a looker, curvaceous, and propelled by a straight-eight Buick engine under its sloping rear end. We called the bus "Big Red", and I thought it was the most modern thing about the school, considering the gothic architecture and some of the thinking by the preppies there. The bus was used for taking school teams to sporting events and transporting the students to and from the Wilmington train station.

At the beginning of fall term, the Pennsylvania Railroad drops me and some classmates off at the station, and there's Big Red. Barry, the bus driver, greets us, "Welcome back to the monastery." We like this guy. We head south on old Route 13 and climb the big steel arch bridge over the Delaware River/Chesapeake Bay canal. At the top, Barry applies the brakes. No brakes. He tries the hand-brake, which snaps and fails. Quick thinking Barry double-clutches down to second, then first gear. It sounds like the transmission is dropping on the road, but it holds, and the engine compression saves us from disaster, slowing the bus down to about 15 mph. We creep along until Barry stalls the engine to a stop at the school. That's the last I saw of Big Red.

UP-ROUTED

In the late 1980s and early 1990s, when I was new on the job, some of my behavior and experiences were examples of things not found in any bus driver's manual. There were probably a few more similar incidents, but they have conveniently faded into fuzzy bus-driving memory.

Anger management, anyone? I'm trying to make a right turn in downtown Northampton, when two guys in a Saab convertible cut me off. Just as the Saab sweeps across the front of the bus, I yell as loud as I can through the open driver's window, "YUPPY SCUM!" Any pedestrian within 100 feet of the intersection must have heard me. My throat is sore for a week. That was the only and last time I yelled anything from a bus.

Miss Manners While I'm driving a local city run, a woman flags me down between two bus stops. Because I'm a nice guy, I pull over for her and say in a friendly way after she boards, "Gee, do you know where the bus stops are?" She barks, "Don't try to tell me anything. Just keep driving!" I keep quiet. After turning the next corner, I drop off the last passenger at a bus stop, except for this woman, then continue on route. She continues to sound off at me. Time to feign a breakdown. I pull over, stop, flip on the four-way flashers, and pull the front door air-release knob, which makes a loud hissing sound, then shut the engine down. "What's wrong?" she asks. "Loss of air-pressure. It could take 40 minutes to get a mechanic out here to fix it." She stomps off the bus. I give it three minutes, then start the bus and continue driving. I see the woman walking along and pull over, open the door, and say, "I fixed it, hop on." On she hops, and all is peaceful.

Go figure One day a guy gets on my bus in Amherst, pays the fare, and then tells me he doesn't like the sound the bus makes. He repeatedly insists on a free transfer for the next bus, figuring it might be quieter. I tell him transfers are only good for transferring to a different route, not for catching a later bus on the same route, so no transfer. Across the street, I recognize the next bus for the route I'm doing. I know that bus has a particularly noisy worn-out differential. I tell the man, "There's your bus. After it turns around, it will be at the stop just ahead in 20 minutes. Have a nice ride." He storms off the bus.

It happened one day My bus, an old Fishbowl (see page 55), is creeping up a long, steep, winding mountain road with no breakdown shoulder, on the way to a community college in Holyoke to pick up a load of students. I have the pedal to the metal doing about 15 mph with the engine screaming away in first gear. Traffic behind the bus is about half-a-mile long. I'm feeling queasy. There is one passenger on board, an elderly woman seated near the front. I turn to her and say, "Lady, I think you may want to move back a little." She asks, "Why?" Then I throw up.

It happened one night One snowy winter night, I am doing a run out of Northampton to Amherst. Just after downtown, the traffic is rerouted left into a side street, due to a building fire. I turn the 40-foot Grumman as directed and figure the next right turn will get me back on route. This street is long and narrow with cars parked on both sides. It turns out to be a dead end, and it's impossible to back out. I mutter incoherent words a few times, and one of the 15 or so passengers asks, "How long we going to be here?" I say, "Maybe all night." They all get off. In front, I see three cars in a yard. I figure the yard is about 60 feet square, and if those cars were not there, I just might get the bus turned around. Soon, several dozen students come out of the apartments. (Back then they could afford to live there, before the old apartments were renovated into expensive condos.) I ask if they have seen this kind of situation before. No, they say, laughing. Three guys come over to move their cars out of the yard. I drive the bus into the yard, and after 20 minutes of forward and backward maneuvers, I get that sucker turned around. I pull out of the yard, tooting the horn for the cheering students as I drive back out of the street, turn right, and eventually get back on route, half an hour late.

It happened another night The main bus stop at UMass is at the end of a narrow one-way entrance with metered parking and a similar one-way exit separated by a large green. One early evening, as I approach a large group of waiting passengers, I stop to let a car ahead of me back into a parking spot, but the car doesn't move. I give two gentle toots with the horn, but the car still doesn't move, so I proceed slowly ahead. Just as the bus almost clears the car, the car swings out to back into the parking spot, striking the side of the bus near the back. I stop, call dispatch, and soon the UMass police show up to investigate. I hand the proper paper work to one policeman, while another policeman yells, "Get out of the bus!" I turn around to see what passenger the policeman must be addressing. Policeman says, "You, the driver, get out of the bus!" I shut the bus down, ask everyone to get off, then I do the same. All the waiting passengers walk over to see what's going on. The police officer tells me to walk behind the bus, where I see two squad cars along with backed-up traffic that has no room to pass. I'm ordered to do a complete sobriety test! So picture this: Here I am, wearing the bus uniform, doing the nine heel-to-toe steps, forward and back, standing on one leg counting out loud, placing my index finger on my nose with eyes shut, and all the rest of the test. Then I hear what must have been a more senior officer say, "He's OK," and finally the accident is documented. I get back on the bus and tell everybody who wants to board to walk up to the nearby bus stop where I can pull over and let the backed-up traffic pass. As the students board, one asks me if it's safe to ride my bus. I tell him he should check with the UMass police. I hear another nicer person say that this is the most bizarre incident she has ever seen. I never found out the probable cause for justifying the sobriety test. I wrote it off as, to put it politely -- stuff happens.

And it happened yet another night I'm driving the late-night shift with just two college girls and one bleary-eyed man on board. Bleary Eyes keeps complaining because he says he consumed a whole case of beer at a party. A student suggests a six-pack or two, maybe. They joke about it, ribbing Bleary Eyes. Just thinking about the topic makes me want to pee, so I pull off the highway next to an all-night Dunkin' Donuts to use the restroom. I shut the bus down, with the four-way flashers and interior lights on, and ask the college girls to sit tight, I'll be right back. Bleary Eyes is fast asleep. When I walk out of the restroom, the college girls are at the counter, drinking coffee. I tell them to put the lids on the drinks and bring them along. A few bus stops later, I wake up Bleary Eyes near some apartments where he lives. Arriving at Amherst College, I have a ten-minute wait before proceeding to UMass. I recognize an Australian accent from the two students, talking about nondescript mainstream American beer. I ask them if they have tried some of the local brews. They have not. I recommend a few. I tell them I hear Aussies like their beer warm. Some do, they tell me. Repulsive, I say. Time to pull out. Just as I'm making the turn into downtown Amherst, one of the college girls jumps onto my lap, putting her hands on the steering wheel, and gleefully announces "I've never steered one of these things before!" I yell, "WHOA, WHOA!" and she hops off as quickly as she hopped on. It's all I can do to keep from laughing as I suggest she shouldn't do that again. It's one in the morning when I drop off the Australians at a nearby university dorm.

PASSENGERS

Our busiest route is between Northampton and UMass/Amherst, carrying mostly college students. To them, anyone over 30 is of a different species, and since I'm over 50, I must be from a different planet. That's OK because I don't have to communicate much. I just try to drive the bus right, smile when people board, maybe say, "How you doing?" Little pleasantries are fine. The idea is to be cool, friendly, and professional, keeping a low profile. On other local routes, many passengers know each other, and generally there's plenty of camaraderie. Some of the regular passengers and I are on a first-name basis. It's easy for a bus driver to get drawn into some kind of discussion about, say, sports, but I keep comments to a minimum. Considering what the general public does when driving, like text messaging, it's amazing how easily a driver can be distracted just by having a discussion. I'm convinced that every accident on the road is caused by driver distraction and not paying 100% attention to driving. Any minor scrapes I have had in the past were precisely for that reason.

Once, when I started bus driving, my body language must have expressed some annoyance because at the next bus stop, a passenger remarked, "I hope you have a better day tomorrow." I soon learned to control the body language. A disgruntled bus driver might think sympathy is deserved because of an annoying situation, but really, the driver is setting him or herself up for humiliation. Consider this: these days, if a passenger perceives unprofessional service, that person can take a picture of the bus driver and the bus number with a cellphone camera, and e-mail it along with a few mean words to customer service and even to the press. This could be uploaded on YouTube before the bus reaches the next stop.

The bus driver might be the first person an upset passenger sees at the beginning of the day. A friendly greeting from the driver can do much to defuse the passenger's bad mood. Bus driving can be a stressful job at times. But as with a lot of jobs, especially ones dealing with the general public, there are options for minimizing stress, which will make the job easier. If a passenger becomes argumentative because the bus is late, I don't get drawn into any discussion. I hand the person a bus schedule with the phone number and suggest he or she take it up with the company. If I'm more than five minutes late, I report it on the radio to dispatch, so it's documented.

I ignore kids who are loud unless they're using offensive language, in which case I pull over at the next bus stop, secure the bus, and walk back to the offending kids, make eye contact, and ask them in a calm voice to cut the bad language.   Some kids stare incredulously, because they're not used to being told not to do something. When they see 30 pairs of passenger eyes staring at them, they get quiet fast.

Not sure if the right fare was deposited? Maybe I didn't pay attention to the "amount deposited" readout before the next fare was dropped in, so I ignore it. It's silly to question a passenger, if the driver is not sure. If I know the fare was short, I ask the passenger to deposit the correct additional amount. If a passenger is not familiar with the fare system and doesn't have additional change, I ask the person to make up the difference next time riding a bus, although usually another passenger will come up and deposit the extra dime. Sometimes a person will board and then fumble for change at the bottom of a backpack. This can take awhile. I suggest it might be a good idea to have the fare ready before the bus shows up.   I don't show annoyance, leaving that up to the other people waiting to board. Occasionally, two youths get on at the mall and deposit less than the correct fare. I look up and say they're short 70 cents, and one will say, "That's all we got." I tell them we'll be on our way after they pay the right fare. Typically they come up with a dollar bill and deposit it, demanding the 30-cents change. Sorry, no change. If they still don't pay the correct fare and walk to the back of the bus, more time is wasted. I have to secure the bus, walk back, and ask them to come up with the money or I'll call dispatch who will call the police. So far in my experience, a fare issue has not come to that point. However, the loud-profanity issue did once.   The profanity got so loud and constant, in spite of my telling the person to cut it out, I had dispatch arrange a reception for the offender in Amherst center. There, a policeman escorted the person off the bus.

One day, traveling on an open stretch of road towards Easthampton just after a rain shower, I see an astounding double rainbow. I just had to pull the bus over onto the shoulder and stop, announcing, "Folks, get a load of that double rainbow." They were as amazed as I was. A good three minute show.

The vast majority of people are decent and reasonable.   Often, passengers, including students, say "Thanks for the ride", or give a friendly wave as they leave the bus.

TRAFFIC

Bus driving, dealing with passengers, and lousy traffic are all part of the job. The driver can control the first two but not the third. Most motorists are considerate, but some are not. Sometimes, while trying to pull out from a bus stop with left-turn signals on and a red traffic light just ahead, cars approaching from behind will not let you pull out, even though they can't continue because of the red light. After the light changes to green, you try to ease out, and usually some kind soul will let you, but if not, you're stuck with another red-light cycle. Often, a not-so-kind soul will pass, only to hit the brakes immediately in front of the bus and make a right turn into a strip mall. Motorists don't like to be behind buses. Not so long ago, this dislike was justified because not until the 1990s were transit buses designed to route the diesel exhaust out at the top of the bus instead of at the bottom. Previously, the dirty, smelly exhaust was aimed directly at the vehicle behind the bus. Motorists, including me, would do anything to get around a bus. What took so long mandating top-routed exhaust, especially for federally-funded transit buses? Actually, diesels are a lot cleaner-burning now that the sulfur has been eliminated from the fuel.

A bus driver could have another career as a traffic engineer, or at least as a consultant to one, because there is plenty of time to see how traffic flow could be improved. Traffic lights could be better synchronized. Left-turn through signals could be reprogrammed to allow more than five cars to make the turn from a left-turn lane filled with 20 cars backed up, blocking the fast lane. Really, it's not rocket science. The congested and unattractive Route 9 highway in Hadley is challenging, but for visual relief, there's the sight of the nearby Holyoke Range.

1957 BUS TRIP

Half way through my college sophomore year in Providence, my uncle invites me to Lincoln, Nebraska, for the Christmas holidays. With my part-time job and the reasonable rent of seven dollars a week, I can swing the $38 round-trip Greyhound fare to mid-USA. The night before the trip, at the old bus terminal, an impassive ticket man prints out the entire round-trip ticket. It is series of foldable perforated segments, about three feet long. Each segment is an individual ticket for one scheduled stop to the next. Upon leaving each stop, the driver tears off the segments for the next stage of the trip. It takes a while for the clattering machine to print out this accordion paperwork. Ticket man says, "That's $38.78." I proceed to write a local check. Ticket man says, "Cash only." I see no sign about cash only and tell him I'll be back with cash in the morning. Ticket man has even less expression as he slowly tears up the long ticket. Next morning, before my final class, I get the cash from my bank and then the ticket. These were the days before credit cards and long before ATMs. I'm back at the terminal for the midnight bus to New York City.

A dual-engined Scenicruiser rolls in from Boston. I see a half dozen license plates on the front. Decades ago, public carriers had to have a plate for each state travelled.

The driver tears off the first five segments of my ticket (New London, New Haven, Bridgeport, Stamford, and New Rochelle). I board along with five other night riders. The Boston passengers are snoozing. The driver restarts the bus as one engine turns over, trying to start the other engine through a fluid coupling. (See **Bus Dynamics** for technical details.) With both engines running, we pull out, never shifting into top gear until leaving Rhode Island and getting onto a recently completed section of the Connecticut Turnpike. We go only 20 miles before barricades direct all traffic to a secondary road to New London, then it's old US Route 1 all the way to the Big Apple. I sleep till 3 a.m., when we pull alongside the bus depot in Bridgeport with a neon sign flashing "BUS" along with the running legs of the greyhound. I see factory workers inside an all-night cafeteria, having 3 a.m. breakfasts after their night shifts – a scene Edward Hopper could have painted. One person boards. I doze off, waking up as the bus rumbles along Bruckner Boulevard in the Bronx towards Manhattan, then over to Ninth Avenue at 110th Street. The traffic lights are beautifully synchronized heading down Ninth. The driver simply idles the bus along at a constant 20 mph, crossing each intersection just as the next light changes green, one after the other, all the way down to 34th Street, 75 blocks away. We pull in under the veranda of the Greyhound terminal on 34th between Eighth and Seventh Avenues. I retrieve my Samsonite suitcase and put it in a self-storage locker for ten cents. Nearby is the magnificent 1910 Penn Station, shamefully torn down in 1963. Its beaux-art architecture is separated by just 25 years from the streamline modern architecture of the bus terminal, itself torn down a few years later.

I hear the cacophony of New York City waking up at 5 a.m. as I walk over to the nearby New Yorker Hotel for breakfast, where I'll meet my brother who is joining me for the rest of the trip.

About 7 a.m. we board another Scenicruiser bound for Pittsburgh. After pulling out of the Lincoln Tunnel beneath the Hudson River, we enter the New Jersey turnpike heading south in the Jersey Meadowlands and see the spidery three-and-a-half-mile-long Pulaski Skyway crossing both the Passaic and Hackensack Rivers. The bus pulls off the Turnpike for a stop in Newark, then heads west on US Route 22, stopping in Bethlehem/Allentown. "Scenics" were equipped with a restroom at the bottom of the steps to the top deck, but stops were made at roadside diners at meal times. We pull over to one about 30 miles west of Allentown. The bus dwarfs the diner. What I liked about traveling 50 and more years ago was the chance to appreciate the particular character of local places. The sameness of corporate chains had not yet taken over the country. Eating and sleeping accommodations were primarily family-owned. Things were beginning to change, though. The first Holiday Inn opened in Memphis in 1952, and the first McDonalds franchise appeared a year later. As we roll along the Pennsylvania Turnpike, I see the stone facades of the Howard Johnson restaurants dating from 1940 when the first 160-mile section of the turnpike opened. Late afternoon we pull into Pittsburgh, smoky from the nearby blast furnaces. There was talk about cleaning up the pollution, but few anticipated that this would solve itself within the next four decades with the near collapse of the American steel industry.

With an hour to kill, my brother and I stretch our legs before boarding the same bus with a different driver for the overnight trip to Chicago. Stops are Cleveland, Toledo, and South Bend. It's pouring rain as we head back to the turnpike on McKnight Road, an old four-lane highway with heavy traffic, the main north portal out of Pittsburgh. It's a steady climb up from the Allegheny and Monongahela Rivers as we grind along, passing within inches of tractor trailers, one after another, the blur of rain spray obliterating everything. Our driver is good. The Pennsylvania Turnpike merges directly into the recently completed Ohio Turnpike. After a quick bite at the huge Cleveland Greyhound terminal, I manage to get some sleep, waking up as we cross the rough streets of industrial South Chicago. I see the almost-completed Chicago Skyway on the left. When I ask the young lady across from me if she has slept well, she says "Nein." She's German, coming to the States to marry a doctor in Fargo, North Dakota, after a correspondence courtship.

We watch the dramatic Chicago skyline from Lake Shore Drive until the bus goes underground into the terminal. My brother and I take in a noontime matinee movie, *The Sweet Smell Of Success* with Burt Lancaster and Tony Curtis.

Late afternoon, we board another Scenicruiser, an overnighter to Omaha. We head out on Cermak Road through Cicero and ten other contiguous municipalities for about 30 miles. The driver downshifts and upshifts the whole way, one block and traffic light after another. I see plenty of street life. The December weather is mild; kids are playing on the sidewalks, and older folks – many, I imagine, born in Eastern Europe – are sitting on porches. The silver Scenicruiser must look impressive to those older folks if they can remember what transportation was like 50–60 years before.

The year 1957 was the end of an era. By that time, the construction of Eisenhower's ambitious interstate highway system was underway. These new highways also intruded on vibrant and familiar neighborhoods with their corner grocery stores and movie houses. People knew their neighbors back then. But it wouldn't last. Buying a big car and moving to a brand new split level house got too appealing. Many of the older – and poorer – people stayed on their porches and became lonely for the vibrant life they used to watch on their streets.

Out on the plains, the bus stops at a rural dirt crossroad to let off a farmer who had some business for the day in Chicago. His family is waiting for him in an old car parked on the dirt road. Long-distance buses used to stop anywhere someone wanted to get off or on, called flag-stops. The movie, *North By Northwest*, features an amusing flag-stop scene just before the airplane crop duster spectacle.

It's night as our bus driver slowly shifts up through all six gears to a cruising speed of 70 mph on the narrow concrete highway. Someone is softly strumming a guitar.   Both engines are humming away, creating a resonance that lulls me to sleep. I wake up in Omaha. What's Omaha without a steak breakfast? We board a late 1940s Silverside for the final one-hour leg to Lincoln. A cold front is moving towards us, and soon we're in a snowstorm.   It will be a white Christmas in Lincoln, but not before I see a couple of Burma Shave rhymes.

> Drinking drivers
> Nothing worse
> They put
> The quart
> Before the hearse
> *Burma shave*

> Is he lonesome
> Or just blind
> This guy
> Who drives
> So close behind
> *Burma Shave*

THE CREW

The Northampton bus operation is part of a larger group in Springfield which, in turn, is contracted by the PVTA to operate all public transportation in the Pioneer Valley. (Learn about transit authorities in **Bus Dynamics**.) Our garage has 50 employees consisting of 35 drivers, about half full-time, half part-time, and three additional standby drivers, four mechanics, one wash-bay man, and four managerial personnel including two dispatchers, the chief mechanic, and the general manager. As bus operations go, the Northampton garage is a small one, with about 17 transit buses. Most are 40-footers along with a few 35 and 30-footers. The drivers are a diverse lot, ranging in age from mid-20s to mid-70s; about 30% are women. Three of the mechanics, including the chief, are from the old country, so Polish is what I hear in the three-bay shop area. They keep the buses rolling, doing everything from replacing light bulbs to heavy engine and transmission work.

The full and part-time employees drive assigned routes, as explained in a previous chapter. The three standby drivers have no assigned routes but are called from time to time to drive a variety of routes, which they can accept or decline. All full and part-time drivers, the wash-bay man, and the three mechanics are in the UFCW union and have benefits, though there are far fewer benefits for the part-timers. Standby drivers are not in the union and have no benefits. When I came aboard in 1988, I worked part-time for 2 years, full-time for 8 years, then, with social security kicking in at age 62, went back to part-time for 8 more years. At 70, I accepted a standby position, choosing to work about 15 hours mid-week during college semesters and less during the summer. It's good flex-time work.

In 2003, I was asked by the part-time drivers to represent them in the upcoming negotiations with the Springfield management for a new union contract. I was happy to do so. Earlier, I had researched information showing that the cost of living was higher in Northampton than Springfield, yet the Springfield drivers had a higher hourly rate. Same work, equal pay, we in Northampton reasoned. Over the course of the existing contract, the full-time drivers did achieve the same pay gradually, in steps over a six-year span. However the maximum part-time pay was frozen at 80% of the full-time pay. With the new contract, I figured the part-timers should also get the same hourly rate. Remembering what I had done for the full-timers about cost of living, the full-time shop steward supported my position.

Negotiations were conducted at the UFCW Local 1459 office in Springfield. Before getting down to business, the union representative handed out paperwork on standard procedures, including proper conduct. I noted that shouting, name calling, profanity, or any acts of disruption would not be tolerated. Oh?

In the early days of negotiations, issues – apart from pay – were quickly settled. The part-time pay issue, however, went on for several months. I knew part-time pay would never equal 100% of full-time, even though some part-timers work close to a 40-hour week, but we pushed for that anyway. Finally, management offered 82.5%. More weeks went by, and 85% was offered. Management said there just wasn't the money to offer more, but we kept plugging, once until three in the morning, with unlimited coffee. Finally I suggested a compromise: "We'll meet you halfway, how 'bout 90%?" The response: "No, no, we can't do it." Two weeks later, the union representative asked me to meet him at a Northampton location, where he informed me management agreed to 87.5%. I said, "Done deal", shaking hands. I'm convinced that an equitable settlement was reached because we were all reasonable and respectful of one another, both management and the drivers. In a later contract, in the summer of 2010, the 90% goal was finally achieved for the part-timers. I was not involved because I was no longer in the union, having switched to standby status four years earlier.

The only time I see most of the drivers is at drivers' meetings, which management holds several times a year. I see some of them as we crisscross each other on the highway when a friendly wave is expected. My wave is a subtle right-hand rise about two inches above the steering wheel. If I see the same driver later en route, I don't keep waving. Occasionally I accept an early route, reporting at 5:00 a.m., when I get to chat for a few moments with some drivers and maybe one of the mechanics. During the day, drivers kill time in the ready room before their next route assignment. Topics range from the state of states' bankruptcies to dumb traffic situations and to the least favorite passenger of the week. All topics kicked around in the ready room are kept strictly to ourselves; no passengers ever enter that room. For more than two decades, I have enjoyed the camaraderie at the garage.

THE COACH, TRAINING AND TRIPS

Training   In the early 1990s, I'm asked if I would like to do some charter-coach work, and I say sure.   The company owned eight coaches. Five of them were 40-foot General Motors buses built in the mid-1970s, updates of the GM Scenicruiser built 20 years earlier. Known as Buffalos because of the stepped-up roof near the front, they had an aesthetic appeal for me, though not quite as much as the Scenicruiser. (See more about bus style in **Bus Dynamics**.)

A few other drivers and I board a coach with the garage manager, who will give us some tips on how to handle the four-speed manual transmission. This proves to be a tricky procedure because the rod linkage from the floor-mounted shifter extends nearly 40 feet back to the transmission, and the gears are not synchronized. The manager drives the coach a short distance out of town to a lightly traveled rural road and pulls over. He asks who wants to go first, and one of the three trainees volunteers. Better he than me to grind the gears, which he succeeds in doing quite well. It's my turn next, and I grind my share; I also have a tendency to slam my left foot down hard on the clutch pedal while double clutching. The manager tells me I don't have to punch a hole in the floorboard. The third guy tries and does a good job, grinding the gears only once. We all take turns for about an hour, traveling about 40 mph, constantly downshifting and upshifting between third and fourth gears. We're getting pretty good at it, driving the coach up and down the rural road.

So, what's with the gear changing? To down-shift into a lower gear or up-shift into a higher one, the clutch is disengaged, the transmission is shifted into neutral, the clutch is re-engaged, and the accelerator is quickly tapped to get the engine to the speed it will be in the next lower or higher gear. Then the clutch is disengaged again, and the next lower or higher gear is selected and finally the clutch is re-engaged. Got that? It's fun. Called double-clutching, it has to be done just right and quite quickly, otherwise there's gear grinding. Done wrong, the bus has to be brought to a stop, then shifted up through the gears again.

I drive the coach back to the garage, where manager man tells us he thinks we can handle the shifting well enough to take a coach out to practice on our own time. This I do between transit split-shifts, driving the coach in city traffic then out to River Road north of Hatfield up to Deerfield. For lunch I pull into the nearby Whately Diner, a truck stop.

A couple of days later, I take a coach up to Leverett, where I live, parking the bus next to the Congregational Church opposite Town Hall, then walk to my nearby house for lunch. The next day I try out a Canadian-built Prevost coach. The starting procedure is different from a GM coach, but I figure it out, leave the bus property, and head up to Leverett again, parking by the church. My wife tells me nobody can figure out who's parking tour buses in the center of town. I finish the sandwich, walk back to the bus, and try to start it. It doesn't start. A combination of switches has to be turned in a particular sequence to start the bus, but I forget the sequence. I have to get back to the garage 15 miles away for my afternoon transit run so I call the garage telling them of the stranded coach, then have my wife drive me to the garage. The reception there isn't pretty. It wasn't till early evening that they got a couple of guys out to Leverett to retrieve the coach. Later my wife tells me that some town people are not happy about old coaches parked in the town center.

Coach Trips I did about half a dozen local charter coach trips before the coaches were relocated from the Northampton property. One of the more interesting trips was to take the entire UMass Minuteman Marching Band up to Brattleboro, Vermont in 1991. This requires five Buffalo coaches for nearly 200 players with their instruments. The occasion is the celebration of Vermont's 200 years of statehood. At about seven in the morning on a brisk clear fall Saturday, we pull in at UMass and pick up the happy players, who stow their instruments in the underfloor luggage compartments. An hour later we drop them off in downtown Brattleboro, then park the buses at a high school, about a mile away. The drivers want to see the parade, so the five of us hike back downtown just in time to see the start. From any vantage point, the parade goes on for a good three hours, followed by a performance by the best university band in the country, the UMass Minuteman Marching Band. The sidewalks are packed. Afterwards we hike back to the school, where the UMass players and bus drivers are treated to dinner and a knockout performance by the band at the outdoor school stadium. Half of Brattleboro is there, giving thunderous applause when it's over. We pile back into coaches, arriving back at UMass about nine that night.

Another time, a seasoned coach driver, Wally, calls me to ask if I'll do a charter job he wants to get rid of. Details, please, I ask. Pick up a load of women at the Hotel Northampton and take them to a fancy restaurant in a rural area, about 30 miles away. These women fly around the country to experience gourmet dining. "Will this restaurant feed me in the kitchen while the ladies feast?" I ask Wally. Of course, he says, and adds the ladies like to tip the driver. Neither happens. I'm in no mood to entertain the ladies on the way back to Northampton, my humor not good because of an empty stomach. The most I can muster, as we pass south of Amherst, is to announce on the intercom, "If you look right, you will see the twinkling lights of Amherst." Dead silence. I hear someone muttering about a weird bus driver.

An interesting experience related to me by another coach driver is the time he took a load of high school kids up to a resort in Sherbrooke, Canada, during Christmas vacation. He parked the bus near the main building, and enjoyed the resort food, fun, and a good night's sleep. Early next morning he stepped outside. No coach. The big parking lot stretches about 150 feet away with a slight down-slope, and as he scans the scene, muttering stuff, he sees the 25-ton coach way down at the bottom of the lot. Apparently black ice was beginning to form when he parked the night before, and that was just enough to carry the coach gradually down the slope throughout the night. No harm done. Fortunately no other vehicles were in the coach's path during its nocturnal creep.

I'm glad I had the coach experience. Those non-synchronized manual-shifting General Motors buses were the last of the breed. Today's coaches are all computerized automatics. The Buffalos were the last coaches made by GM, with production ending in 1980.

2010 BUS TRIP

I notice a full-page advertisement in a bus trade magazine at the garage announcing "The Hounds of the Mother Road" reunion taking place in Adrian, Texas. This was to be a reunion of surviving privately owned Scenicruiser buses built by General Motors in the mid-1950s. The Mother Road is the old US Route 66, and Adrian, population 150, is the exact midpoint of that highway that ran between downtown Chicago and Santa Monica, California.

A reunion of Scenicruiser buses? Naturally I had to go, wouldn't anyone? A cheap airfare gets me to Amarillo, where, at the Big Texan Steak Ranch, ten Scenics and three other 1950s and '60s coaches roll in. Tom, from Peoria, illinois, was an organizer of the event and owns a beautifully restored Scenic with its original Greyhound paint scheme. He welcomes me to ride with him to Adrian the next day.

Next morning we pull out, rumbling through the historic section of Amarillo on old Route 66 and out to Adrian, 45 miles west. The folks there at the Mid Point Cafe are waiting for us. This cafe has been a meal stop for long-distance bus passengers since the 1930s when Route 66 was built. Though no longer a bus stop because of nearby Interstate 40, the cafe is still operating, encouraging motorists and truckers to take the Adrian exit for a good meal and a slice of its famous Ugly Crust Pie. We pull up to the cafe, while the other buses turn off the highway opposite the cafe, making a slow turn on a Texas Panhandle field to angle-park facing the north side of the road. It is a sight to see those beauties lined up. About 85 people riding the buses, many of these folks known in the bus industry, stroll into the cafe for lunch. I pick some brains about Scenicruiser mechanical idiosyncrasies. After lunch, we cross the road to check out all the buses and talk with the owners. Looking back at the cafe, I see Tom's gleaming Scenic with a man in vintage Greyhound uniform by the door "collecting" tickets, a scene from 55 years ago. Heading back to Amarillo, the buses pull off the highway at Cadillac Ranch, a revered site of ten '50s and '60s Cadillacs half buried nose first into the ground. Late afternoon, we arrive back at the Big Texan. That evening we enjoy a banquet and a slide presentation about Scenicruisers and Greyhound history. I pass on the free 72-ounce steak (free if consumed in one hour), settling on a nine-ounce filet mignon. No one in our party ordered the six-pound steak, but there were photos on the wall of customers, including slender looking women, who had. I thank Tom and his wife. She's the one who encouraged Tom to acquire the 55-year-old Scenicruiser.

a pair of Scenics at the Mid Point Cafe

GRANDMOTHER'S BUS TRIP

My grandmother loved to see the country by bus. This was decades before the era of "tour" buses. She traveled by regularly scheduled Greyhounds and other regional lines. In 1955, she even took a bus all the way to Alaska on the Alcan Highway built during WWII. Here is an excerpt from her account of a bus trip taken in the southwest in the late 1940s.

> This Santa Fe, it is like no place else on earth. You feel like you are on top of the world, the sky so close, if ever, in touch with the infinite? I had only intended to stay a few days, but the spell of this place holds me. Glorious warm sunshine, the sky so blue with masses of white clouds. I shall never forget the first time I came. The bus suddenly topped a rise and there below was the great flat tableland, the Taos valley spread out to the already darkening mountains, sacred mountains snow covered, shining in the golden glory of the sunset. The white clouds have turned to grey – the "Rain God" coming with great strides, marching majestically over the mountain and plain, giving rain joyously there in answer to the good Indians' prayers.
>
> New Mexico, west out of Albuquerque. The shower of welcome rain makes the road ahead a glistening silver ribbon leading to a golden sunset under the masses of grey storm clouds. North from Gallop on the Cannon Ball Bus Line. Through the Navajo Reservation for miles the road goes through desolate desert. Suddenly two fantastic mountains, sharp pointed, rise up ahead. We stop to take on some Navajos at Little Water Trading Post. Ahead now is a long flat table mesa against the sky and another strange rock formation like a great cathedral. The bus driver points out "Shiprock" and the little town ahead named for this goliath of the desert sea. How terrifying this rock mountain must appear on a moonlight night. The bus driver slows down for a narrow bridge. It would be fun to take it at high speed. Beyond Farmington the country changes. Across the state line following the Animas River a tiny tumbled down adobe house in the village of Bondad. Suddenly the road climbs seemingly to the top of the world. Still climbing, the mountains getting higher, in the distance a still taller range – the backbone of

the Rockies against an angry sky. The wind blows and the sawtoothed mountains are wrapped in clouds of dust, their sharp outlines barely visible against the horizon. From Las Cruces going west on a good road crossing the desert, one looks out on little hillocks covered with curious green vegetation, prickly, forbidding. Dark blackish rocks dot the desert and sharp leaved yucca are everywhere – beautiful in bloom. The vegetation changes, the desert flattens out and in places a sort of grass blows gently in the wind, a pale sulphur color as the sun, filtering through the dust clouds, shines on it.

Winding now through a canyon the road is narrow and perhaps the driver is wise to continually blow the horn. A bus ahead of us broke down and our driver stops to help. I think a "plug" came out of some part of it. I heard our driver say "They stuck a pencil in it and it's going." Remarkable what those Greyhounds can do!

BUS DYNAMICS

INTRODUCTION

This part of the book is heavy on bus detail. You have to be some kind of bus-nut to want to read it. Remember, at the beginning, about the circle check? You get the full-boat details of that here. What's a transit authority? Explained. What about the buses I drove? It's all here. And what's this about Scenicruiser idiosyncrasies? Read on. Ever lie awake nights thinking of bus styling? That's here, too.

THE CIRCLE CHECK

If this chapter reads like a manual, so be it.

Paper work Upon showing up for work, you'll pick up the details about your particular route, or "run". There could be more than one run, a split shift, for that day. The time sheet is filled out with the date, your signature, badge, bus and run numbers, plus the start and end times of each run. This weekly information is fed into the payroll department computer and at the end of the following week, you'll get a paycheck. A defect card is filled out at the end of each run showing any bus defects that may have occurred during the run. Make sure the schedule racks on the bus are filled with schedules for all the bus routes in the system. Required paper work that must be with you at all times includes the CDL (commercial driver's license) and the Medical Examiner's Certificate. You'll need a card listing all bus company management phone numbers. If a bus breaks down at 2:00 a.m. you'll use the bus radio to give the nighttime dispatch, located in a different city, the local chief mechanic's home phone number.

Start the bus You will be assigned a bus number, and you'll find the bus with that number. Turn on the battery switch, then turn a knob in the driver's area to the "run" position, making sure the air-actuated parking brake knob is on and the automatic transmission is in neutral. Flick another switch or push a button to start the engine. Flick yet another switch to make the engine run faster. That's the "fast idle" which ensures proper engine oil circulation.

Lights Turn that run knob one more position to switch on the outside and interior lights. Turn signals are controlled by a pair of floor-mounted push-button foot switches; a blinking light on the dash will show the switches are working. Flick another switch to turn on the four-way flashers.

Air pressure gauge The air pressure gauge on the dashboard is an important instrument. A transit bus weighing close to 20 tons can carry more than five tons of people, so stopping that bus effectively is, how shall I say, crucial. When a bus is started, the engine runs an air compressor which feeds air into two separate systems, each with its own pressure tank located under the bus. A gauge will show air pressure building up to the correct pressure of 120 psi (pounds per square inch), and it is this air pressure that activates the brakes. The compressor automatically kicks on when air pressure drops to near 85 psi and kicks off at 120 psi. If one system fails, the other will function as a backup, but the bus should be removed from service until both systems function perfectly. If pressure falls below 85 psi in both systems, the engine will shut down automatically. There is an override switch to restart the engine just enough to get the bus off the road. Loss of pressure is automatically transmitted to dispatch through the radio system. Large vehicles have room for the air compressor with pressure tanks, and besides, that air is out there for the taking. Air is also used for pumping up the air-bellows suspension (a smoother ride than leaf springs), transmission activation, opening and closing doors, and a few other things, like the windshield wipers. It's reassuring to hear that hissing sound the air makes when braking a heavy vehicle. Buses built during the last 20 years are equipped with a retarder device that allows the engine compression to do much of the braking, saving wear and tear on brake shoes.

Mirrors The mirrors on the front outside corners of the bus are an extension of the driver's eyes. It may seem scary to drive anything that doesn't permit you to see out a rear window with an interior mirror; but with a bus, or any big rig, those outside mirrors work well after some practice. They should be adjusted so that when you are comfortably seated in a normal driving position, you can just see the bottom of the rear tires. There are little convex mirrors within or attached to the regular mirrors. These are the "fisheye" mirrors that show a wide-angle view away from the sides of the bus that the regular mirrors don't show. If all looks clear from behind before pulling out from a bus stop, double check that fisheye mirror at the same time. A car might be driving out from a gas station across the street heading straight for the mid-section of the bus.

Program the destination sign and fare box There are code numbers and letters to be punched into the destination key pad for lighting up the front and side signs for both outbound and inbound destinations, including the route number. If you forget to do this, waiting passengers don't smile as you approach the stop. Button "A" lights up the outbound destination and button "B" lights up the inbound destination. Another key pad attached to the fare box has to be programmed with the driver's badge, route, run, and trip numbers. A run number is the driver's assignment, which might be, for an example, five round trips or five loops. When a bus starts out from the first bus stop, it is headed outbound to a destination, which is trip one. When the bus returns, it is headed inbound, which is trip two. The next outbound trip is trip three, and so on. So if a bus is doing five round trips, it is doing ten trips, five loops, and one run. The driver must punch in the next trip number each time the bus turns around. If you forget to punch in the trip numbers and an average of 30 passengers traveled on the bus for each of the ten trips, the passenger count will show three hundred passengers carried on the first trip. No bus is that big, except in the movie *The Big Bus*.

While driving a route, the driver will key in the number and category of passengers picked up at all stops. Categories include: full fare; reduced fare for the elderly, disabled and children 12 years and under; infants at no fare; students who have the correct student card at no fare; transfer requests; wheelchair and bicycle pickups. New transit buses have bicycle racks attached to the front that can carry up to three bikes. If all this seems confusing, it will become second nature after a short time on the job. The reason all this information is coded before and during the route is so transit management can know how many and what category of passengers rode the bus for each trip at any time of day or night. Every day, all this information, along with the money, is extracted from the fare boxes of all the buses and documented by computer. Over time this information is used to determine if route adjustments should be made and, it is hoped, if ridership is increasing. Constant and accurate data collecting has to be done to justify continued funding for public transportation.

Driver's seat The seat can be adjusted in a variety of ways as in a car. Adjusting the driver's seat so it is just right will make it easier for you to concentrate. Full-time attention to safe driving is a must while driving a bus. If you are not comfortable and your back aches, you will not concentrate well. It was not so long ago that bus manufacturers did not design driver's seats very well, and many seasoned bus drivers ended up with back problems.

Passenger buzzer Flick another switch to turn on the passenger buzzer (or chimes). You don't want a passenger yelling from the back of the bus, "Hey, that's my stop you just passed, the buzzer's not working!" What's nice about newer buses is that the buzzer will sound only once until the door is opened, so the driver doesn't hear the buzzer ring repeatedly before the next stop.

Climate control Flip the climate-control switch. Depending on the outside temperature, either heat or air conditioning is controlled by a thermostat. On nice temperate days, leave the climate-control switch off and open the roof hatches for fresh air circulation. On most buses, passengers can slide the windows open a little.

Continuous loop camera Check to see if the continuous loop camera is working, shown by a green light near the dashboard. If a button next to the green light is pushed, a wide-angle camera will record anything that has happened near the outside of the bus, front, sides, and rear, as well as the interior. The camera will capture what occurred before and after the button is pushed. The recorded evidence will show what really happened if a motorist side-swipes a stopped bus but claims the bus pulled out while the car was passing. Many cases have been resolved in the bus company's favor thanks to the continuous loop camera. Trouble could occur inside the bus, like an intoxicated passenger harassing others. The bus driver has to be alert enough to push the button when trouble occurs so that it is documented.

Passenger seats and stanchions Check the passenger seats and stanchions to make sure they are secure, not loose. Stanchions are those poles standing passengers hold onto. Without something to hold onto, a standing passenger will fall, no matter how gentle the ride.

Horn Test it.

Wheel chock, fire extinguisher, warning triangles Make sure these items are in their appropriate storage areas. If a bus breaks down, the triangles are placed on the road behind the bus to warn approaching motorists. A wheel chock is placed against a front wheel if the driver is off the bus, even though the bus is shut down with the air brake on. In the unlikely event there is loss of air pressure, the chock will prevent the bus from rolling.

Is the bus floor swept and trash removed? If not, tell dispatch. The previous driver will be docked some pay. Go ahead and sweep the bus and get rid of the trash. There are trash containers on board for passenger convenience.

Wheelchair lift and kneeler Every federally funded transit bus manufactured since 1990 is equipped with a wheelchair lift (or ramp) and a kneeling device, as required by the Americans with Disabilities Act (ADA). The kneeler lowers the front of the bus about six inches to make it easier for elderly and disabled passengers to board and exit at the front door. Make sure these devices are in working order, using the appropriate controls. Three connected inward-facing seats on both sides of the bus flip up to provide room for wheelchairs to be parked with securement devices.

Lights Check the headlights, four-way flashers, marker lights, and brake lights. Marker lights are those small red lights at the top front and top rear of the bus. Each side has an amber marker light at the bottom in the middle of the bus. Brakes and brake lights are automatically on when the rear door is opened so the bus cannot move while people are getting off using that door. No, you do not slow down a bus by opening the rear door.

Tires Give all the tires, including the inside rear ones, a good swift kick with your hard-toe uniform-issued shoe. Tires will feel hard if properly inflated and soft, if not. If your toes hurt because you're wearing sneakers, you're out of uniform. Check all the wheel lug nuts to make sure they're not loose.

Body panels Look for any body dents, cracks, and scratches on the bus, especially scratches on the right outside mirror housing. In winter, body damage might be along the bottom edge of the side, caused by turning too close to a frozen snow bank. Any fresh damage should be reported to dispatch, who will check to see if the damage has been documented. If it has not, dispatch will photograph the damage and document it. The previous driver will be held responsible. If you do not report the new damage before taking the bus on the road, you will be held responsible. Bus companies deplore damage because it raises a safety concern about the driver.

Engine coolant Open a small flap near the engine compartment to check for green liquid engine coolant in a sight glass. If this liquid is not visible, there is insufficient coolant, and the engine will overheat. Before the engine is damaged due to overheating, the engine will shut down automatically. Dispatch will know because that information will be transmitted through the radio system, as with the loss of air pressure.

Radio Pick up the handset of the radio. Press a button on the handset to talk and release it to listen. You will say your bus number and request a "10-5," which means, "is the radio working?" Dispatch will say "10-6," which means the radio is working. You acknowledge by saying "10-4." If a passenger wants to transfer to another bus which could be missed by a few minutes, you can call that bus by its route number and request that it wait up to five minutes. In a serious situation, such as a bus breakdown or an accident, you can switch the radio from "all call" to "dispatch" so only dispatch hears the message; no need to broadcast details for passengers to hear throughout the entire system. The number "10" followed by another number represents a specific message commonly communicated between dispatch and drivers or between drivers. Once the radio 10 codes are understood, communicating is concise, saving time and unnecessary words. Additional examples of codes are: 10-2, repeat the message; 10-7, driver is out of the bus (nature calls); 10-8, driver is back on the bus; 10-10, bus is in service; 10-13, bus is overloaded, cannot pick up more passengers; 10-15, driver change (another driver takes over the route at the end of the previous driver's shift); and 10-17, behind schedule, usually due to traffic congestion. A driver might say to dispatch, "10-17 11 UMass inbound," meaning: "leaving UMass 11 minutes late, returning back to Northampton, due to traffic congestion." Other codes are 10-20, location of bus; 10-23, wheelchair passengers; and 10-24, bicycles on the bike rack. Dispatch documents all 10-13s, 10-17s, 10-23s, and 10-24s. Naturally, some messages have to be communicated with words, but those words should be kept to a minimum. Dispatch is a busy person and does not need chatter. Communicating personal stuff on the bus radio can lead directly to a pink slip. A driver using a personal cell phone while driving a bus means prosecution, a big fine, and never driving any bus again. If the radio fails and the driver must communicate with dispatch due to an emergency, a cell phone may be used, if the bus is stopped and secured.

In the fall of 2010, new radios were installed, hooked up to a GPS system that changes the destination sign at the end of each trip without driver input, counts the number of people boarding with a photo-electric eye, and automatically announces major stops. The radio/GPS system knows everything it has to know about the route by the driver's badge and run numbers programmed by the driver into the display before leaving the garage. Waiting passengers can call a number with their cell phone, tap in the bus route, like B43 for the Northampton/UMass-Amherst route, and be informed exactly when that bus will be at the stop the person is calling from, even if the bus is late.

Fixing minor defects before starting the route If something can be quickly corrected, such as a burned-out light bulb or low engine coolant, let one of the mechanics know. The mechanic will stop the job he is doing and replace that light bulb. If the radio is not working, dispatch will loan you a portable one. If there is something significant that cannot be corrected within ten minutes, you'll be assigned another bus and get to do the circle check all over again. You'll be a little late, but it will not be your fault. If everything checks out, the whole circle check can be done within five to seven minutes.

TRANSIT AUTHORITY

Up through the Second World War and into the early 1950s, urban public transportation was a reasonably profitable business, but as affluence increased during the next decades, people bought cars and moved out to new suburbs. Privately owned public transportation began to feel the financial pinch as ridership fell. Increasing fares and eliminating routes only made things worse. Transportation advocates knew that if there was no public funding, public transporting would simply cease to exist. By the early 1960s, publicly funded agencies called transit authorities began to be formed to manage public transportation in metropolitan areas throughout the country. The challenge was how to pay for new buses, pay to operate them, and pay wages. Operating costs alone amounted to more than what was collected in the fare box. So in 1964, the Federal Government set up an agency under the US Department of Transportation called the Urban Mass Transportation Administration (UMTA), later changed to the Federal Transit Administration (FTA). This agency grants transit authorities 80% of the cost for new buses. The 20% balance comes from state revenues. Operating costs were another matter. At first UMTA paid a portion of that, but as those costs kept rising, the Feds said "no more." Thereafter, what the fare-box did not cover was raised from local and state tax revenues. To this day, it is always a struggle raising the cash to keep public transit running. Sometimes transit authorities have to borrow money and pay interest to the bank, then beg the state for reimbursement at the end of the fiscal year. Indirectly, the taxpayer pays that interest. When the economy is down, there is less tax revenue, so the financial situation is worse, despite increased transit ridership which, by 2010, has approached 1950s levels in some urban areas. But even with the financial difficulties, transit authorities have improved the quality of public transportation over the past several decades, although not up to European standards. In Europe there is a higher level of political commitment for excellent public transportation, particularly inter-city high-speed rail.

Sadly, the two major US transit bus manufacturers, General Motors and Rohr/Grumman/Flxible, terminated bus production in the late 1980s, in spite of their huge investments in the design, tooling, and production setup for the new RTS and 870 series buses (see the next chapter). Production was sporadic because of insufficient demand for transit buses. Often, the states had (and still have) a hard time coming up with their 20% share. The business climate is not the best for those still supplying transit buses for the US market. This will change when there is a greater political commitment for excellent public transportation.

In most major metropolitan areas, transit authorities own and operate the buses. In other areas, transit authorities own the buses and contract with private companies to operate them and pay wages. Private companies specializing in transit operations submit bids to transit authorities, and the lowest bidder gets the job, assuming that the company is qualified. The company that hired me back in 1988, Western Mass Bus Lines, was a local company under contract since the 1970s by the Pioneer Valley Transit Authority (PVTA) to provide more frequent service with new UMTA-funded buses. Previously, the company ran a limited service between Northampton and Amherst/ UMass with old transit buses and even school buses converted for transit duty. In the early 1990s, Western Mass Bus moved to a different location, concentrating on charter coach work. The Northampton operation eventually became Valley Area Transit under Springfield Area Transit, both contracted by the PVTA.

Also in the 1970s, another entity, UMass Transit, run by the University of Massachusetts, was contracted by the PVTA to serve the Five College area, with routes between the University and Amherst, Hampshire, and Mt. Holyoke colleges along with another one between Smith and Hampshire, plus other towns near Amherst. All the drivers and dispatchers for this service are students. Some move on to transit-management careers. Over half a dozen different managers I have worked under over the years at the Northampton garage started driving transit buses at the university during their student days.

THE BUSES

I drove several types of transit buses, as illustrated in this chapter starting on the next page. Following are design and mechanical backgrounds about these vehicles.

After the transit authority expanded to the Northampton/Amherst area, the old buses were scrapped, and brand new 35-foot transit buses were soon on the routes. These futuristic-looking vehicles, known as the RTS (Rapid Transit Series), were made by General Motors. Additional 40-foot buses were made by the Grumman Corporation, owner of Flxible, also a venerable bus manufacturer. Both the RTS and Grumman designs evolved from a government-funded program in the early 1970s known as "Transbus." People with disabilities (such as those confined to a wheelchair) rightfully put pressure on the government, arguing that as long as public transportation was funded with tax dollars, all modes of such transportation had to be accessible to the disabled, the elderly, and anyone in a wheelchair. So, UMTA initiated the Transbus program, inviting bus manufacturers to submit proposals to build drivable low-floor "Bus of the Future" prototypes, paid for with federal dollars. They were hand-built, then evaluated, but none of these prototypes went into production. There were problems with the Transbus specifications along with other issues. For one thing, the small wheels would not have endured the rigors of everyday service. The Transbus program was shelved and eventually the prototypes were scrapped.

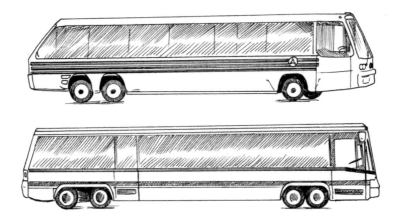

GM (top) and Rohr Transbus prototypes

The practical solution for making a bus accessible was to provide a lift for wheelchairs, along with a pneumatic air-operated kneeling device for lowering the front of the bus at stops. That technology existed in the 1970s, but it wasn't universally implemented until 1990, almost 20 years later, when the Americans with Disabilities Act finally required all new publicly funded buses to be accessible for the elderly, disabled, and those in wheelchairs. What evolved from the Transbus program, though, was the futuristic styling of the RTS transit bus. It was put into production in 1977 and was the last bus designed and produced by General Motors.

GM RTS

In addition to the GM RTS buses, our garage had half a dozen 40-foot Grummans, the 870-series transit bus, which also evolved from the Transbus program when Rohr Industries owned Flxible. Rohr sold its bus operation to Grumman Corporation in the late 1970s just when the 870 series started production at the Flxible plant in Ohio. At that time, the New York Transit Authority bought nearly a thousand of them, with the usual 80% Federal funding from UMTA. But it was not long before cracks developed in the "A" frames that supported the rear axle. All those buses were towed to the Grumman military aircraft plant on Long Island, where a special shop was set up to reinforce the frames. As the buses were returned to the MTA, further problems with the frames developed. There are usually two sides to an issue. The MTA did not practice good preventative maintenance in the 1970s and early 1980s as evidenced by the graffiti-covered subway cars and buses at the time. In any case, while lawyers got rich over the frame issue, all MTA Grumman buses were removed from service and stored. The MTA had to pay back UMTA the initial 80% cost of the buses, less depreciation. Eventually, most were sold off cheaply. New Jersey Transit bought many of them and experienced no significant problems. Additional MTA 870 series Grummans were sold to other transit authorities, including six to the PVTA which assigned them to the Northampton garage. I liked driving them; they had a floaty ride, like my aunt's 1953 Buick.

Grumman 870

Why is "Flxible" not a typo? Before Flxible started making buses in the 1920s, it made motorcycle sidecars connected to motorcycles with a flexible device. This enabled the motorcycle to lean when cornering, while still keeping the sidecar tire in contact with the road. In registering "Flexible" as a trademark, the sidecar company learned that the S.L Allen & Company had already registered that name for their Flexible Flyer sled, so the "e" was intentionally removed, and the trademark was registered as The Flxible Company. The "misspelled" name was a clever ruse because people thought twice about it.

Previously I mentioned that a transit bus weighs 20 tons. Yet a 40-foot bus has only about 270 horsepower, about the same power as a V-6 medium-sized sedan. How can the bus move? Torque, not horsepower, is what counts. A big heavy diesel engine has plenty of torque, about 800 lb-ft (pound-feet), compared to a sedan's gasoline engine with about 200 lb-ft of torque. Engine torque is a *turning* force that turns the crankshaft. Those big pistons in a diesel engine with 800 lb-ft torque can easily turn the engine crankshaft with enough force to move the 20-ton bus. Unlike higher-revving gasoline engines, where horsepower is more significant, the relatively slow-turning diesel engine has lots of low-speed power. Because of the huge forces (high compression) within a diesel engine compared to a gas engine, diesels are heavy and extremely rugged. If properly maintained, they can go up to a million miles before a major overhaul.

General Motors favored two-stroke diesels for buses, rather than the usual four-stroke type, because the two-stroker has a better power-to-weight ratio, thus more power with a smaller and less complex engine. In a two-stroke engine, the piston is fired down every time it's at the top position, instead of every other time as in a four-stroke type. A two-stroke diesel engine sounds as if it is running twice as fast as a four-stroker, but it really is not. It's the fired power strokes that occur twice as often. The disadvantage is that the two-stroke engine puts out more pollution because of the way the exhaust is scavenged out of the cylinders. With tighter emission regulations, GM buses built since the early 1990s no longer have two-stroke engines. I miss the smooth, rhythmic sound of the two-stroke diesel compared to the chugging agricultural sound of the replacement four stroke, four cylinder 40-foot RTS buses delivered in the mid-1990s. But there might be a future for the two-stroke diesel engine. With sophisticated electronic management, it is possible that pollutants can be controlled so that the advantage of the two-stroke diesel engine is realized again.

By the mid-1930s, the angle-drive system was perfected for bus applications. To explain, the rear engine with the transmission is installed crosswise, not lengthwise of the bus, with bevelled gears taking the drive shaft to the differential at the center of the drive axle. Because an engine is narrow compared to its length, the front-to-rear space for the engine area can be less than if the engine and transmission were installed lengthwise. The advantages of the angle-drive were increased passenger capacity, better engine accessibility for maintenance, and less rear overhang with a longer wheelbase for increased underfloor baggage capacity. The angle-drive would remain a GM bus feature, except some 1940s coaches which were powered by the shorter four cylinder engine installed lengthwise and the Scenicruiser coach which used a pair of those engines.

Since the late 1930s, General Motors set the best mechanical and style innovations for buses. Yet, by 1987, GM was out of the bus-manufacturing business. After a ten-year run with the RTS transit, GM sold off the rights to assemble that bus. It continued in production under other name plates for another decade. (Also, GM sold off EMD, the Electro Locomotive Division, in 2005.)

I drove another bus called the Fishbowl, built in 1966, a model that was produced from 1959 through 1977. It was powered by a V-6 configured two-stroke diesel instead of the straight six cylinder as previously used. The windshield, made up of six pieces of compound curved glass, was the largest windshield on any bus at the time, hence the Fishbowl nickname. The bus was also known as the New Look bus to distinguish it from its predecessor, the Old Look GM TG/TD transit bus, which entered production in 1940. More than fifty years after the Fishbowl entered service, it's still the New Look bus, even though it has been out of production since 1977. The one I drove was numbered 1302, not the usual 7000 series at the Northampton garage, because it was on permanent loan from the Springfield folks. We used it on the Easthampton and Holyoke Community College run until it was finally retired in 1993 after nearly 30 years of faithful service. It had a two-speed transmission which reminded me of the '71 Chevy Vega (a horrible car) I used to own with its two-speed tranny.

GM Fishbowl

Starting in 2007, new buses were delivered to the Northampton garage, replacing most of the aging RTS units. The new buses are made by Gillig in California with Cummins turbo-charged, four-stroke, six-cylinder diesel engines. Cummins is the only American diesel engine manufacturer left supplying engines for heavy-duty transit buses. Unlike the drive system previously used by GM, where the engine and transmission were installed crosswise, the Cummins engines and transmissions in the Gilligs are installed lengthwise, resulting in a long school-bus-type rear overhang. When those buses were first delivered, I was not the only driver who managed to smack the rear-end of a Gillig into a wrought-iron waste receptacle installed right at the curb, while pulling out from a busy bus stop in Northampton. When pulling out, the rear of the bus swings over the curb opposite the steering direction.

The Gilligs are up-to-date in terms of function, with a low floor in front, and no front steps for easier boarding. The low floor is possible, thanks to a front drop-axle design. With the kneeling feature, the front of the bus can be lowered to almost curb level, so that a passenger can simply walk on. The only steps, located behind the rear door, are for the rear section of the bus, raised to clear the drivetrain. The Gilligs have a much improved wheelchair ramp at the front door, instead of the troublesome folding rear door steps that converted into a wheelchair lift on previous buses. Actually, the bus does what the Transbus program tried to achieve in the mid-1970s. The Gilligs are OK to drive, but they sure could use a little style.

Gillig

THE SCENICRUISER

General Motors made 1001 Scenicruisers exclusively for Greyhound between 1954 and 1956 (see page 65). Styled by Raymond Loewy, the coach was a split-level design, and was the first 40-foot-length coach allowed to operate in every state.

The drivetrain was unique. There were two engines in the back, both driving through a fluid coupling into a three-speed manual transmission. Each of the three speeds operated through a two-speed "splitter," an overdrive for each of the three forward gears. In effect, the bus had six forward speeds. All six speeds had to be used to maximize the torque and power of both engines in getting the Scenicruiser up to highway speed. The splitter was engaged by an electrical solenoid switch operated by the driver between each manual shift. The reason for this complicated drivetrain system with the two engines was that General Motors did not yet have an engine powerful enough for the Scenicruiser. The straight six-cylinder diesel engine (as opposed to the "V" cylinder arrangement, which came later) was powerful enough for the 1940's-era Silversides (also styled by Raymond Loewy in the late 1930s) but not for the bigger 40-foot buses. So, the decision was made to install a pair of four-cylinder engines, side-by-side and lengthwise of the bus, connected by the fluid coupling, to provide a combined output of about 300 horsepower. Unfortunately, that coupling device could not take the stress of many thousands of miles of operation, causing Scenicruiser breakdowns during scheduled revenue service. Greyhound was not happy. Right from the start, this whole drivetrain setup was problematic. It was impossible to keep the speed of the two engines in perfect synchronization, which played havoc with the fluid coupling, thus failure. With today's microcomputer management, the engines could have been kept in sync, but that kind of technology did not exist in the 1950s.

So, it was the beginning of the end of a long-established relationship between General Motors and Greyhound. In 1961, Greyhound bought Motor Coach Industries (MCI), a Canadian coach manufacturer, and began to make its own coaches. MCI eventually became independent of Greyhound and is now a US-owned corporation but with primary production still in Winnipeg, Manitoba, and a smaller assembly plant just across the border in North Dakota.

By the end of the 1950s, GM had developed a V-8 diesel which had more than enough power, but declined the job to retrofit the dual-engined Scenicruisers. Because Greyhound was committed to those coaches, it turned to a heavy equipment outfitter, Marmon-Herrington, to pull out the four-cylinder engines with the troublesome transmission system and replace them with the single V-8 engine, installed lengthwise, with a straight four-speed transmission. Retrofitted Scenicruisers continued to operate for Greyhound until the mid-1970s when they were finally replaced by buses not made by the General. The Scenics were sold off to smaller operators, a few remaining in service 40 years after rolling off the production line in Pontiac, Michigan.

I learned about the Scenicruiser drivetrain one cold January night in 1961. Bound for Providence from New York City, the bus broke down before leaving the Bronx. The driver provided no explanation, perhaps complying with company policy. The man I was sitting next to moaned "That fluid coupling." I said "What?" He told me all about the drivetrain problem. A Highway Traveler (page 64) was dispatched to picked us up a couple of hours later. That Scenicruiser was probably one of the last due for the new drivetrain.

An issue brought about by the US Justice Department in the late 1950s could be considered one more nail in the coffin for the Coach Division of General Motors. The politicized issue was that there were those who did not like the idea that GM manufactured coaches, like the Scenicruiser, exclusively for one carrier. In any case, by 1980 General Motors chose to get out of the coach building business. Today, no heavy duty coach is 100% engineered, tooled, and made in the United States.

two radiators, one for each engine

BUS STYLING

Today, almost no one riding a bus gives two hoots what the bus looks like. But there was a time when American buses had great style and character. This was especially true of General Motor buses. My enthusiasm about buses stems from the style they used to have.

The era of good style for public transportation, the streamline era, began in the mid-1930s and lasted into the 1970s. Since then, as specifications and funding for transit buses moved into the federal arena, away from the private sector, captivating bus style has disappeared. Generics and severe functionalism have replaced good style. But I believe there is no reason why good style cannot be incorporated with function as it once was. Sure, it would be silly for the Federal Transit Administration, the agency that funds 80% of the cost of new transit buses with taxpayer money, to specify anything about style. However, bus manufacturers should just provide good style – gratis.

Unlike transit buses operated by public transit authorities, large intercity coaches and tour buses are operated by the private sector, so there is no government funding for those vehicles. MCI is a major coach supplier and the Prevost coach is imported from Quebec. Other large coaches are European imports. Importers gush about "Euro Style". There is no longer an "American" coach style.

Following is an historical account of the style of the American bus, both the intercity coach and the transit bus.

Coach styling I refer to General Motors because, by the mid 1930s, it really set the standard for bus style for the next 40 years. Here's a little background about the General Motors involvement with buses. In 1915, a gentleman by the name of John D. Hertz started a taxi outfit in Chicago called the Yellow Cab Company. The color yellow has since become synonymous with cabs. This is the same Hertz who started car rentals. In 1923, Hertz also got into the bus building business and named it the Yellow Coach Manufacturing Company. A few years later, General Motors took note and acquired a majority interest in Yellow. A new plant was built in Pontiac, Michigan, where Yellow Coach and GM set up a large bus manufacturing operation. With the expertise of both entities, the modern bus design and drivetrain developments were in high gear by the mid-1930s. These developments included the angle-drive layout and perfecting the two-stroke diesel engine, both referred to in a previous chapter. With the engine in the rear, the front of the bus could be flat, without the engine sticking out front as with previous buses. This made room for styling opportunities. With sheet-metal curvature, a bus could be given some eye appeal.

While Yellow Coach/General Motors made a variety of coaches for any number of carriers, Greyhound specified several exclusive coach designs for itself and its affiliates (carriers feeding into the Greyhound system). The first such coach was the Model 719 Super Coach, production beginning in 1936. The Super Coach set the design parameters for all future coaches. The passenger level was higher to allow for underfloor baggage, instead of baggage stowed on the roof covered by a tarpaulin. Initially the engines were gasoline, before the two-stroke diesel was produced in the late 1930s. Transmissions were still manual. Standard air conditioning and on-board restrooms were features yet to come, 20 years later. From a styling standpoint, the 1936 Super Coach was well proportioned and looked bigger than it really was because of the small side windows. But I never liked the goofy swooping white paint scheme flowing above the wheel wells.

1936 Super Coach

The next Yellow Coach design, again for Greyhound, was the curvaceous Silverside, the Model 3701 series styled by Raymond Loewy, industrial designer extraordinaire. This coach made a hit when displayed at the 1939 New York World's Fair. Older folks at the fair, remembering travel by stage coach pulled by a team of six horses, must have been impressed by this coach. No swooping paint scheme for this baby; Loewy specified fluted-aluminum siding, a style influenced by those wonderful streamliner trains entering service during the 1930s – hence the name Silverside. This siding feature would continue for future GM coaches and for coaches made by MCI into the late 1980s. About 600 pre-war Silversides were built for Greyhound and its affiliates, first with gas engines, and subsequently, with the new straight six-cylinder, two-stroke diesels. Oddly, the manual shift lever was mounted on the steering column. The linkages from the shift lever back to the transmission in the rear must have been quite interesting.

1940 Silverside

In 1939, Yellow Coach produced a small coach called the Cruiserette, with a gasoline-powered rear engine. Stretched versions of that bus, the 2900 series, with a 160 horsepower four-cylinder, two-stroke diesel engine were produced in the early 1940s. A pair of those engines would power the big Scenicruiser a decade later.

stretched
Cruiserette

Another coach, a taller version of the 2900 series to accommodate under-floor luggage, was the 3301 series made in 1942. It featured the British RAF red, white, and blue "bull's eye" insignia behind the head of the leaping Greyhound. This was to honor the British who, with a handful of Spitfire fighter planes, prevented the Luftwaffe from bombing England into complete submission in 1940 during the famous Battle of Britain. These coaches were known as the "Battle of Britain" buses. Many late 1930s Super Coaches were repainted the same way.

1942 Battle of Britain Coach

In 1943, GM bought Yellow Coach outright, and from that point the General became the bus meister of the industry. The Pontiac plant was busy turning out a variety of coaches and transit buses before the war, and it was a lot busier after the war. In 1948 GM produced 2000 more of the pre-war designed Silversides for Greyhound, and produced the Model 4101 for other carriers. These re-styled coaches had the same drivetrain as the Silversides, but without the fluted metal siding.

Three years later, GM came out with the 4102/3 series coach, an updated Silverside, most with full-fluted aluminum siding. Fifteen hundred were built between 1951 and 1952, many sold to Trailways. At one point during the production run, the aluminum siding was not applied due to the short supply of alloy during the Korean conflict.

1951 updated Silverside

Other coach manufacturers were busy, notably ACF-Brill (favored by Trailways), Kenworth, Aerocoach, Spartan, Beck, Fitzjohn, MCI, and Crown Coach, which evolved into the current Gillig Corporation, maker of today's transit buses. Most notably, there was Flxible with its well-styled curvaceous rear engine Clipper model, first produced in 1938. The front cover of this book shows a pre-war Clipper with a post-war paint scheme. In 1940, the Clipper got a neat-looking air scoop on the roof near the sloping rear end for engine cooling, and, after the war, a more rounded front end. In my opinion, the Clipper was the prettiest bus made.

1948 Flxible Clipper

In 1953, GM introduced the 4104 series coach called the Highway Traveler, the first completely re-styled coach in the postwar period. Other coach manufacturers copied the new GM styling theme, but not quite as well. The major technical improvement was the suspension. With no more leaf springs, this new coach rode on air for a smoother ride. It used air bellows, the air constantly replenished by the air compressor. Transmissions were still manual and would remain so for all future coaches made by GM. An onboard restroom was an option, and, finally, air conditioning became standard. The same Silverside-era straight six-cylinder diesel did the pushing, but did not have enough power to drive the air conditioning compressor at the same time; so an under-floor small gas engine did that job. Some Silverside predecessors had the same air conditioning setup. Fully clad with the characteristic metal fluting, including front and rear, the Traveler had a design cohesiveness that worked well, a styling theme that was thoroughly modern, bright, and well-proportioned, with the windshield slanted just right. The most recognizable new visual element was the larger passenger windows, slanted to give the bus a sense of forward motion. This slanting window design and the full metal cladding would remain a GM coach feature until the last one produced in 1980. The 4104 series was produced for seven years until 1960 when GM updated the styling with the 4106 series. The major mechanical change was the installation of the more powerful V-8 diesel which eliminated the need for the small gas engine to drive the AC compressor.

1953 Highway Traveler

The most impressive GM coach was the 40-foot Scenicruiser, the third and last coach built exclusively for Greyhound. The style of this split-level coach evolved from a 1949 running prototype designed by Raymond Loewy. That prototype was put into scheduled service while Greyhound was trying to get all states to allow 40-foot coaches, an achievement finally realized in the early 1950s. The unusual drivetrain system was discussed in the previous chapter, and from that, we know GM did not always get things right. But the General certainly got the styling right, with its own in-house design team, Raymond Loewy's oversight, and input from Greyhound. The gleaming visual look and impressive proportions of the Scenic were features one would have expected from a confident America of the 1950s.

1954 Scenicruiser

Trailways, Greyhound's smaller competitor, wanted a 40-foot coach, but of course, could not get the Greyhound Scenicruisers. Beck built just 12 copies of the Scenic, and Trailways took three of them. To increase their 40-foot coach fleet, that carrier had no choice but to turn to Europe because no one else in the US made 40-footers. In 1957, Trailways chose Karl Kassbohrer, a German bus builder. Four years later, Trailways set up a new plant in Belgium, where these coaches were made to Trailways' specifications with GM's new V-8 two-stroke diesels installed crosswise. In the mid-1970s the entire operation was moved from Belgium to Brownsville, Texas. The revised Trailways coach produced there had a more Americanized style. Called the Eagle series (next page), they were produced into the 1990s.

1980 Trailways Eagle

The final GM coaches were the 35 and 40-foot Buffalo series, which continued with the characteristic GM coach styling theme of the fluted aluminum siding and the slanted passenger windows. The drivetrain was the same as the retrofitted Scenicruisers, except that the engine was installed crosswise, as with usual GM bus practice.

1966 Buffalo

But the era of iconic American bus style was coming to an end. Beginning in the 1960s, MCI became a major coach manufacturer for the US market. Later in that decade, it was producing 40-foot coaches for any carrier. But in my opinion, MCI has never pulled off the styling panache that GM mastered so well. In the late 1980s, I was driving on I-95 in Connecticut and saw up ahead what I thought was a painted 18-wheeler box trailer. It turned out to be a new coach with a squared-off, zero-styled rear end. It's still true with today's buses, that chopped rear end. I know the air conditioning equipment is located at the top rear of buses and a completely squared-off shape will maximize that space. But any competent industrial designer could design the rear end of today's buses with some semblance of style while still providing for the function requirements.

And how has the styling evolved for the small coach lately? Not well, sad to say. The small coach today is a truck with the engine out front with a passenger body mounted on the truck frame, like a bus one hundred years ago. Compare today's truck-bus to the styling of the 1950 "Baby" Flxible Clipper.

early twentieth century   early twenty-first century

mid-twentieth century Flxible Clipper, a good-looking small coach

What I find tiresome, and frankly, a styling cop-out, is the in-your-face riotous plastic film applications of crazy colors all over the sides of buses, especially those tour coaches. They feature swirls, stripes, huge brush strokes, exploding stars – you name it. If these vehicles were not so slab-sided and sharp-cornered and had some degree of visual sophistication in their overall shape, the resulting better style would not have to cry out for the applied graphic pollution. Of course, the bus operator has to have the company identity on the vehicle. I point to what Greyhound has done with its new coaches. They are painted nicely with a combination of blue and light grey, with a minimum of film graphics. The lettering "Greyhound" is exquisite, as it was on the original Scenicruiser in 1954. The dog is the right size, unlike the giant dog used until recently that made the Baskerville hound look like a new-born puppy.

Transit bus styling What about the style of the transit bus? Here too, Yellow/GM set the standard over 70 years ago in 1940 with the TG and TD series, initially gas-powered (TG) followed by diesel (TD). The diesels were the two-stroke straight six-cylinders type, the basic engine that powered most GM transits and coaches, with the exception of the Scenicruiser, for the next 20 years. The short 30-foot TD was powered by a four-cylinder diesel. What was really innovative about these buses was that they were frameless. They featured an aluminum unibody construction for structural integrity. The TDs had a somewhat streamlined look to them, a feature lacking in American transit buses made 70 years later. It was on this type of bus that, in 1955, a brave woman, Rosa Parks, refused to give up her seat for a white man. She was arrested. This incident led to the 1956 US Supreme Court ruling declaring that segregation on public transportation was, finally, unconstitutional.

1940   1959   1977

three generations of General Motors transit buses

The GM Fishbowl transit bus was the next design, entering production in 1959. The Fishbowls were produced for almost two decades, through 1977. These transits had a fair amount of flash, but then, I'll take flash any day over no style. Larger windshields for buses came into vogue in the early 1960s for good reason. To this day, some passengers persist in walking in front of the bus after getting off. The driver can see better what is immediately in front with a large windshield. Flxible copied the GM Fishbowl with its new transits, but didn't pull off the style as successfully.

The last GM transit bus was the futuristic fiberglass-bodied RTS (Rapid Transit Series) which replaced the Fishbowl in 1977. GM built the RTS for only ten years until GM got out of the transit bus business in 1987 and sold off the design rights to another manufacturer. It's interesting to think that the RTS was styled 40 years ago, yet looks so good today. Canadian transit chiefs thought the RTS too futuristic looking for their fellow citizens, so they chose to re-style the old Fishbowl into a more squared-off conservative design called, appropriately, The Classic. As I write this, I continue to drive RTS transits, some over 15 years old. Soon they will be retired, and I'll miss them.

Flxible had its new advance-style transit bus, the 870 series, competing with the GM RTS. Designed and styled by Rohr Industries, an aerospace company, Flxible made them at its Ohio plant. Grumman took over the entire operation, as mentioned in a previous chapter. The styling was original, certainly not a copy of the RTS. More square and less curvaceous, the 870 was still visually impressive (see page 53).

The new Gillig transit buses look, well, severely functional, making no concession to style (see page 56). However, Gillig's BRT series transits do have a more curvaceous front end and a slightly less chopped rear end. Are these styling features gratis? Nope. They are extra-cost options on top of the basic $400,000 bus. Because transit authorities are generally strapped for cash, they are not inclined to pay extra for styling enhancements. Gilligs are the only 100% American-designed and manufactured 40-foot transit buses remaining in the United States. Other transits use Canadian and European designs with satellite assembly locations in the US. With federal dollars paying 80% of the cost of transit buses, there is a 60% US content requirement, so the drivetrains (engines, transmissions, and other components) are American. However, as pointed out in a previous chapter, Cummins is now the only remaining US company supplying engines for heavy duty transit buses. Detroit Diesel, at one time part of GM, is now part of Daimler, a German corporation.

Nearly 75 years ago, the US set the standard for engineering and styling public transportation vehicles. No longer. For the past several decades, we have looked to Europe for coaches, Japan for subway cars, and France for fast-train technology. For super-fast trains, China is leaving everyone in the dust. There are too many Wall Street speculators looking for the quickest possible monetary return at the expense of long-term commitment for what America needs, like updating the nation's deteriorating infrastructure. And the US education system has a long way to go for providing the kind technical skills required for today's manufacturing. It's time Americans are put back to work to engineer, design, and manufacture things America needs. If so, there could be a rekindling of optimism and pride sufficient to re-incorporate good style into American-made transportation vehicles of all kinds, not necessarily retro (though a touch of that may not be a bad thing), but a style that is dynamic and decidedly American in character.

In 1865 (yes, 1865), somebody sketched a streamlined train concept that looked, astoundingly, somewhat like today's high-speed Acela.* Seventy years passed before the streamline style took hold. Seventy more years passed, bringing us to the present time, when the era of curvaceous, streamlined style is all but forgotten.

* Robert C. Reed, *The Streamline Era*, p.23

EN ROUTE

BACK TO THE FUTURE

One hundred years ago, cities and towns were well served by trains, electric interurbans, and street cars. But, by mid-century, the growth of suburbia took off, and the car was the only way to get around in the suburbs. Millions of people abandoned city neighborhoods and public transportation began to deteriorate. Factories began to shut down. By the end of the 20th century and up to the present time, so much of what American used to manufacture is now imported.

The massive highway-building days of the last 60 years are over, even as the US population is projected to increase 100 million by 2050. Traffic congestion around metropolitan areas will become increasingly intolerable. And there will not be enough energy to go around at the rate people are using it today. Continuous conflicts for diminishing fossil fuels will become futile. Environmental damage could be irreversible. We are not on a sustainable route the way things are going. And this from a "car" guy, I would be surprised if private car ownership will exist 100 years from now.

Something has to give. By the beginning of the next century, developments could be quite different, more clustered and linear. Fast, clean, and efficient public transportation would serve these areas well. Future housing, work, recreation, shopping, and industrial activity within each cluster could be located less than a mile from a light rail or a dedicated bus lane connecting a string of similar clusters. The only motorized vehicles within the clusters would be emergency, service, delivery, and public-transit vehicles, all electrically powered. Areas between clusters, perhaps where sprawl previously existed, might be turned back into farmland or open country. The infrastructure for super high-speed rail throughout the country will be in place, with 250 mph trains running dependably on time. These future developments, with plenty of green spaces, would be more self-sustaining and human-scaled than the current faceless sprawl. Electricity would be produced locally, primarily with solar photovoltaics. A grocery store, a corner movie theater, and a community center would be located within walking/bicycling distance or near stops for electric buses circulating within each cluster every ten minutes. Electric cab service would be readily available. Those buses and cabs would be designed and made wholly in the United States. A neighborly spirit in these communities just might regerminate. Such developments might remind people of what communities were like before being completely overrun by automotive traffic.

FLAG STOP

The book stops here, but first some words of thanks. I am especially grateful to Jim and Felicity Callahan with whom I get to have a few beers at a neighborhood pub, the Harp, in North Amherst. Both encouraged me to keep going with this tale. The Harp, by the way, features talented Celtic musicians. My wife, Cynthia, is one of the fiddle players.

The sketch on page 27 was inspired by a Bernice Abbott photograph from the Museum of the City of New York collection, *Changing New York*. The photograph is one of Abbott's many compositions taken throughout New York City in the 1930s. I thank the museum for granting me permission to use that photo as a reference for the sketch. I had the artist update the scene with 1950s buses.

Thanks to Cynthia, who kept me on the right route all along. She resolved many computer wars and never failed to encourage me with her laughter and love.

So long!

Roy Kimmel has a lifelong interest in industrial design, architecture, and all things to do with transportation. He lives in western Massachusetts in a small town with his wife and their rescue dog and cat who, for the record, all have great style.